Rachel Carson

Read These Other Ferguson Career Biographies

Maya Angelou
Author and
Documentary Filmmaker
by Lucia Raatma

Leonard Bernstein
Composer and Conductor
by Jean F. Blashfield

Shirley Temple Black
Actor and Diplomat
by Jean F. Blashfield

George Bush
Business Executive
and U.S. President
by Robert Green

Bill Gates
Computer Programmer
and Entrepreneur
by Lucia Raatma

John Glenn
Astronaut and U.S. Senator
by Robert Green

Martin Luther King Jr.
Minister and
Civil Rights Activist
by Brendan January

Charles Lindbergh
Pilot
by Lucia Raatma

Sandra Day O'Connor
Lawyer and
Supreme Court Justice
by Jean Kinney Williams

Wilma Rudolph
Athlete and Educator
by Alice K. Flanagan

**FERGUSON
CAREER BIOGRAPHIES**

Rachel Carson

Writer and Biologist

MELISSA STEWART

Ferguson Publishing Company
Chicago, Illinois

Photography ©: Bettmann/Corbis, cover; Rachel Carson History Project, 8; Roger Allen Christie/Frances Collin, Trustee/Beinecke Rare Book & Manuscript Library, 12, 18; Rachel Carson History Project, 20; Ferdinand Hamburger, Jr. Archives/Johns Hopkins University, 24; Roger Allen Christie/Frances Collin, Trustee/Beinecke Rare Book & Manuscript Library, 26; Rachel Carson History Project, 31; Roger Allen Christie/Frances Collin, Trustee/Beinecke Rare Book & Manuscript Library, 36, 41; Rachel Carson History Project, 46, 48, 54, 60, 64, 67, 69; Roger Allen Christie/Frances Collin, Trustee/Beinecke Rare Book & Manuscript Library, 73, 78; Bettmann/Corbis, 85; Archive Photos, 91; Ted Streshinsky/Corbis, 93; Bettmann/UPI/Corbis, 98; Bettmann/Corbis, 100.

An Editorial Directions Book

Library of Congress Cataloging-in-Publication Data
Stewart, Melissa.
  Rachel Carson / by Melissa Stewart.
  p. cm. — (Ferguson career biographies)
  Includes bibliographical references (p.).
  ISBN 0-89434-368-8
  1. Carson, Rachel, 1907–1964—Juvenile literature. 2. Biologists—United States—Biography—Juvenile literature. 3. Environmentalists—United States—Biography—Juvenile literature. 4. Science writers—United States—Biography—Juvenile literature. [1. Carson, Rachel, 1907–1964. 2. Conservationists. 3. Biologists. 4. Women—Biography.] I. Title. II. Series.

QH31.C33 S74 2001
570'.92—dc21
[B]   00-049042

Copyright © 2001 by Ferguson Publishing Company
Published and distributed by
Ferguson Publishing Company
200 West Jackson Boulevard, Suite 700
Chicago, Illinois 60606
www.fergpubco.com

All rights reserved. This book may not be duplicated in any way without the express permission of the publisher, except in the form of brief excerpts or quotations for the purposes of review. The information contained herein is for the personal use of the reader and may not be incorporated in any commercial programs, other books, databases, or any kind of software without written consent of the publisher. Making copies of this book or any portion for any purpose other than your own is a violation of U.S. copyright laws.

Printed in the United States of America
Y-3

CONTENTS

INTRODUCTION: CHANGING THE WORLD	9
1 THE EARLY YEARS	13
2 SOMETHING TO WRITE ABOUT	25
3 UNDER THE SEA-WIND	37
4 BUILDING A CAREER	45
5 THE SEA AROUND US	55
6 THE EDGE OF THE SEA	65

7 NEW DIRECTIONS	**77**
8 SILENT SPRING	**87**
TIMELINE	101
HOW TO BECOME A BIOLOGIST	103
TO LEARN MORE ABOUT BIOLOGISTS	110
HOW TO BECOME A WRITER	112
TO LEARN MORE ABOUT WRITERS	120
TO LEARN MORE ABOUT RACHEL CARSON	123
INDEX	125

Rachel Carson

Watching hawks fly overhead. Rachel Carson devoted her life to understanding and protecting the natural world.

INTRODUCTION: CHANGING THE WORLD

Imagine a place where no birds sing on sunny spring mornings, no bees collect pollen on lazy summer afternoons, and no chipmunks hoard seeds for the long, cold winter. This is what Rachel Carson asked her readers to do in the opening pages of her book *Silent Spring.* She wanted them to imagine what could happen if the government continued to spray toxic chemical pesticides over our fields and forests.

Today, we are aware that what we do can affect the natural world. We recycle glass, paper, and plastic. Government officials track and control the amount of polluting substances that are dumped into rivers and spewed from smokestacks. Scientists study global warming and watch for changes in the ozone layer. Environmentalists fight to save endangered species and limit the destruction of their natural habitats. We do all this because we understand that our planet is fragile and that life is precious and rare. We do all this because we do not want to live in a world where no birds sing. We do all this because, in 1962, Rachel Carson wrote a book called *Silent Spring*.

Silent Spring is considered one of the most influential books ever written. Many people credit its powerful message with launching the modern movement to protect the environment. Along with the first views of Earth from space, *Silent Spring* made people begin to realize that we must protect and preserve our world and the creatures that share it with us.

Rachel Carson is best remembered as the demure, intelligent, petite, and driven author of *Silent Spring*, but she also wrote three other best-selling books that described the oceans and sea life. *Under the Sea-Wind, The Sea Around Us,* and *The Edge of the Sea* contain rich, poetic portraits of ocean creatures and enlightening accounts of the interdependence of living things in a natural community. These books also explain how all living things are affected by weather, soil conditions, and other aspects of their environment. This way of thinking about the natural world was new to most people when these books were written. Carson's ideas inspired scientists to develop a new area of study called ecology—the study of living things as part of a natural system, such as an ecosystem or biome.

After her second book, *The Sea Around Us,* was published in 1951, Rachel Carson was acknowledged as a literary genius. But when the chemical industry realized the negative effect that *Silent Spring* would have on their business, however, they tried to discredit her. They called her "a hysterical woman" and claimed that she was "un-American." Rachel did not take the praise or the criticism too seriously, however. She loved science and she loved writing and, no matter how the world reacted to her work, she remained committed to putting down on paper her thoughts, dreams, and passions.

Time outdoors. Rachel (center) enjoyed being outside with her brother and sister.

THE EARLY YEARS

On May 27, 1907, Maria Carson gave birth to a "dear, plump, little blue-eyed baby." She and her husband, Robert, named their newborn daughter Rachel, after the infant's maternal grandmother. Rachel was Maria and Robert's third child. At the time, Rachel's older sister, Marian, was ten years old, and her brother, Robert Jr., was eight.

The Scotch-Irish family lived on a 65-acre (26-hectare) farm in Springdale, Pennsylvania. Their small, two-story clapboard house had four large rooms, but no electricity or indoor plumbing. A barn, a garage, a springhouse, a chicken coop, and two outhouses surrounded it. The family kept some chickens, as well as a pig and a horse, but Rachel's father did not consider himself a farmer. He had bought the land as an investment.

Beyond the Carson home lay open pastureland, orchards with dozens of apple and pear trees, and woods teeming with wildlife. Rachel spent much of her childhood exploring these areas. She and her mother often took long walks together and shared their fascination with the beauty of the natural world. Rachel learned birdsongs and the names of flowers. She watched squirrels scamper up trees, chipmunks dart under leaf litter, and deer leap with their young fawns.

The Real World

The magical world of nature that surrounded Rachel at home contrasted sharply with the landscape she saw when the family traveled to the nearby city of Pittsburgh, Pennsylvania. In the early nineteenth century, Pittsburgh had become the center of the U.S. steel industry. The Allegheny and the Monongahela—two great rivers that meet in the city—provided an ideal way to transport iron ore from mines in the Great Lakes region of New York. Barges also delivered large quantities of coal from local mines. Coal powered the giant blast furnaces that smelted iron ore into steel, the perfect building material.

Soot spewed from the tall chimneys of the steel mills day and night, blanketing the city with a thin layer of black grime. The pollution made it difficult for people to breathe and for plants to grow. When freight trains started to carry iron in and steel out of the city, the steel industry expanded—and pollution became an even greater problem.

By 1906, the year before Rachel was born, sixty-two iron and steel works lined the shores of the Allegheny River. Fifty-eight more were scattered along the banks of the Monongahela. In 1909, the chief zoologist at the Carnegie Institute conducted a series of water-quality studies on the Allegheny River. According to his report, "the Allegheny [at Pittsburgh] is utterly polluted, and we have here possibly the greatest variety of pollution of any of the streams in the state."

This describes the Pittsburgh that Rachel knew as a child. Years later, she remembered her mother's wry comment about Pittsburgh's growth and "progress" and the resulting pollution: "Man was making nature ugly for the best of reasons."

As Rachel grew, so did the industry in the Pittsburgh area. The Carsons had bought their large farm in 1900 with the intention of subdividing it and selling off lots, but soon it was obvious that this plan would not be profitable. The area had changed and had lost its appeal—and its value. By the time Rachel was in high school, her hometown was sandwiched between two large power plants—the West Penn Power Company and the Duquesne Light Company. A third company, the Harwick Coal and Coke Company, filled the air with the nauseating odor of sulfur.

The destruction of her beautiful childhood home—and the financial hardship that her family suffered because of it—was a memory that Rachel would carry with her all her life.

Growing Up Poor

Rachel's mother was a strong, proud woman. She had been raised in a financially secure home and was deeply embarrassed that she and her husband could not provide their own children with a similar environment. Maria had been a teacher when she and Robert met, but she gave up her job after they were married. In the early twentieth century, most married women did not work outside their homes; they spent their time raising children and taking care of their families.

Maria did whatever she could to bring money into the Carson household. She sold fruit from their orchards and eggs from their chickens. She also gave piano lessons to local children. Robert worked as a salesperson and also at the West Penn Power Company, but he seemed to have trouble finding and keeping a job. He had always hoped that the family could support itself by selling land and was disappointed when this plan did not work out.

Even as a young girl, Rachel sensed her mother's embarrassment about the family's financial situation—and she felt embarrassed too. Maria rarely invited other people to their home. She made few friends and did not participate in many local activities. Rachel followed her mother's example, and rather than finding other children to play with, she stayed close to home.

Rachel and her mother spent much time together and shared many interests. They formed a special bond. Maria knew there was something very

Mother, daughter, and dogs. Throughout their entire lives, Rachel and Maria spent a great deal of time together.

special about her youngest daughter. While Marian and Robert Jr. were in school, Rachel had Maria's undivided attention. As a former teacher, Maria knew how to stimulate her daughter's interests and develop her talents. She encouraged Rachel to ask questions and seek her own answers. Often, these answers were found in books.

From a very early age, Rachel read voraciously. Her favorite books included *The Wind in the Willows* by Kenneth Grahame and everything written by

Beatrix Potter. The writing of Potter and many of the other authors Rachel enjoyed as a child featured a love of and respect for nature. These authors also stressed developing the imagination and searching for the truth about the world. These ideas had a profound influence on Rachel's young mind.

Rachel was also enchanted by the lively stories and gorgeous illustrations that appeared in *St. Nicholas Magazine,* a monthly publication that featured the work of prominent authors, such as Mark Twain and Louisa May Alcott, and noted artists, such as Norman Rockwell and Howard Pyle. Years later, Rachel told an interviewer, "I read a great deal almost from infancy and I suppose I must have realized that someone wrote the books, and thought it would be fun to make up stories too."

St. Nicholas provided its young readers with the opportunity to do just that. Besides publishing pieces written by well-established adult writers, the magazine printed stories written by children. In 1918, when Rachel was ten years old, she submitted a story called "Battle in the Clouds" to the magazine. The story was probably inspired by stories her brother had told Rachel about his experiences in the U.S. Air Service during World War I.

An eager reader. Rachel was happy to share a book with anyone, even the family pet.

In Rachel's dramatic story, a Canadian plane is unexpectedly struck by German gunfire: "The plane wavered, and [the brave young pilot] knew that if something was not done promptly, the plane would fall. He saw there was only one thing to do, and he did it quickly. He crawled out along the wing, inch by inch, until he reached the end. He then hung from the end of the wing, his weight making the plane balance properly."

Rachel was thrilled when her story was published—and elated when it won the magazine's Silver Badge, an honor that included a $10 prize. Reflecting on that event years later, Rachel said, "Perhaps the early experience of seeing my work in print played its part in fostering my childhood dream of becoming a writer."

Rachel was not the only well-known author whose dreams were encouraged by publication in *St. Nicholas Magazine*. The earliest stories of E. B. White, the author of *Charlotte's Web* and *Stuart Little*, also appeared in the magazine. F. Scott Fitzgerald, who wrote *The Great Gatsby,* and the poet e.e. cummings both published their first work in *St. Nicholas* too.

The Beginning of a Dream

Over the next year, Rachel wrote three more stories for *St. Nicholas Magazine,* including one that won the magazine's coveted Gold Badge. "A Message from the Front" describes the joy of a group of French soldiers when they learn that the United States has entered World War I. Because the magazine had published four of Rachel's stories within a one-year period, she became an honor member of the St.

Nicholas League. Rachel continued to submit stories to the magazine until 1922, when she turned fifteen.

Buoyed by her success, Rachel began to send stories to other magazines. She soon had her first taste of rejection, but she was determined. She remained a serious student and continued to read avidly. She also began to experiment with poetry.

Because Springdale High School offered classes only up to the tenth grade, Rachel traveled across the Allegheny River to the town of Parnassus to complete her last two years of high school. When she graduated in 1925, the editors of the Parnassus High School yearbook printed this poem about her: "Rachel's like the mid-day sun/Always very bright/ Never stops her studying/'Til she gets it right."

In the 1920s, few men and even fewer women went to college. Rachel's mother wanted the best for her daughter, however. She knew that Rachel dreamed of becoming a writer. Although the family did not have much money, Rachel's parents insisted that she continue her education.

By selling some land at a small profit and pawning the family china, Maria and Robert were able to enroll their daughter in Pennsylvania College for Women (PCW). Now known as Chatham College, the small private school had an excellent reputation and offered a variety of courses. The school was also attractive to Rachel because it had a beautiful wooded campus and was only 16 miles (26 kilometers) from home.

Talented and intelligent. Rachel Carson entered Johns Hopkins University in 1929.

SOMETHING TO WRITE ABOUT

When Rachel began taking classes at PCW, she planned to major in English. One of her professors, Grace Croff, recognized Rachel's talent and determination and encouraged the young student.

Many of the stories Rachel had written for *St. Nicholas Magazine* were about World War I. Rachel now began to write about different topics. One of her earliest compositions for Miss Croff's class was "The Master of the Ship's Light." It describes the experiences of a lighthouse keeper during a treacherous storm. Miss Croff liked the story and wrote Rachel a note that read, "Your style is so good because you made what might be a relatively technical subject very intelligible to the reader." Neither Miss Croff nor Rachel knew it at the time, but years later, this skill would bring Rachel Carson fame and fortune.

The story included vivid descriptions of the sea and shore—a remarkable feat considering that Rachel had never seen the ocean. Everything she knew about the sea came from reading books. Years later, Rachel remembered her early interest in the sea. She told a newspaper reporter, "I was fascinated

Student and teacher. Rachel learned a great deal from Grace Croff (left), a teacher at the Pennsylvania College for Women.

by the ocean, although I had never seen it. I dreamed of it and I longed to see it, and I read all the sea literature I could find." Her reading—and her imagination—had given her an accurate impression of the ocean's rolling tides and the fury of its ferocious storms.

Some of Rachel's other writing efforts focused on her own, firsthand experiences in the natural world. In her second year of college, she wrote the following poem for Miss Croff's class:

> *Butterfly poised on a thistle down.*
> *Lend me your wings for a summer day.*
> *What care I for a kingly crown?*
> *Butterfly poised on a thistle down.*
> *When I might wear your gossamer gown*
> *And sit enthroned on an orchid spray.*
> *Butterfly poised on a thistle down.*
> *Lend me your wings for a summer day.*

A Widening World

During the period in which she wrote this poem, Rachel was beginning to take classes to meet her requirements for graduation. She signed up for biology, and although she did not expect to get much out of the class, it turned out to be a life-changing experience.

The instructor, Mary Scott Skinker, was intelligent and loved teaching as much as she loved science. Her classes inspired many of her students, but Rachel was utterly mesmerized. She learned scientific principles that explained things she had observed while exploring the woods around her childhood home. Many of the seemingly unrelated ideas she had been thinking about for years suddenly fit together like pieces of a jigsaw puzzle.

The students in Miss Skinker's biology class also spent time working in the laboratory. These sessions gave Rachel her first opportunity to view a new part of the world—one that can be seen only through the lenses of a microscope. Again, Rachel was enchanted. The biology class—and Miss Skinker—had such a powerful effect on Rachel that she decided to minor in science.

Because Rachel had made few friends as a child, she initially had trouble finding companions at PCW. Her devotion to biology, however, quickly won her two lifelong friends. Mary Frye was her first laboratory partner. Soon, Mary and Rachel befriended

Dorothy Thompson, a girl who came from a wealthy family and hoped to become a doctor.

Rachel made more friends while working on the college newspaper and after joining a literary club. She played intramural sports and even dated occasionally. Although Rachel was still shy and reserved, she had an active social life and a growing circle of friends. By her junior year, PCW had become a second home to Rachel.

A Change of Plans

In Grace Croff and Mary Scott Skinker, Rachel had found important role models. She continued to take classes in English and biology. She especially enjoyed botany—the study of plants, flowers, and trees—and zoology—the study of animals. In her junior year, Rachel realized that she wanted to change her major from English to zoology. She was concerned that her mother and Miss Croff might be hurt by her decision, but both women supported the change. Rachel continued to work very hard and graduated from PCW in 1929 with high honors.

During Rachel's third and fourth years at the college, she and Miss Skinker had grown closer. In the 1920s and 1930s, there were few opportunities available for women in the field of science, but Rachel decided to follow in Miss Skinker's footsteps. She wanted to earn an advanced science degree. When Miss Skinker left PCW to become a doctoral student at Johns Hopkins University in Baltimore, Maryland, Rachel applied to Johns Hopkins too. She knew that she wanted to become a biologist, but she was not sure which area of biology she would pursue.

Late one evening, Rachel was in bed reading "Locksley Hall" by the English poet Alfred Lord Tennyson. A violent thunderstorm raged outside her window. Just as she read the passage "for the mighty wind arises, roaring seaward, and I go," a lightning bolt lit up the sky and a loud thunderclap echoed across campus. The experience had a tremendous impact on the sensitive young woman. Years later, she retold this story and then said to her audience, "I can remember . . . my intense emotional response as that line spoke to . . . me . . . to tell me that my own path led to the sea—which then I had never seen—and that now my own destiny was somehow linked with the sea."

When Rachel told Miss Skinker about her interest in the sea, the teacher arranged for her protégée to spend the summer of 1929 at the Marine Biological Laboratory in Woods Hole, Massachusetts. When

Discovering the sea. Rachel spent an important summer in Woods Hole, Massachusetts, in 1929.

Rachel arrived at the laboratory, she saw for the first time what she had read—and dreamed—about for so many years: the ocean. Rachel's summer on Cape Cod helped her to clarify her goals. She would put her first love—writing—on hold and devote her life to the study of the sea and its creatures.

Moving to Maryland

Rachel's parents could not afford to pay her tuition at Johns Hopkins. Their financial situation was worse than ever. Rachel's sister, Marian, and her two young daughters were now living at the Springdale farm because her husband had left her. In addition, the family still owed money for Rachel's education. The United States was in the middle of the Great Depression, and jobs were hard to find.

With Miss Skinker's help, Rachel received enough money from Johns Hopkins to make the school affordable. To earn some extra money to help her family, Rachel also worked as a research assistant in one of the school's labs. She soon realized, however, that her small salary was not enough to make ends meet. During her second year of graduate school, Rachel took fewer classes and found a job teaching zoology at the University of Maryland in College Park.

Despite Rachel's efforts to earn money, her parents were still having financial problems. Her mother's stress weighed heavily on Rachel. The two women had always been very close, and living apart was difficult for both of them. Rachel missed her family and suggested that they sell the farm in Springdale and move closer to her. She also thought that her father might have an easier time finding work in the Baltimore area. They agreed, and Rachel found a house they could rent in the town of Stemmers Run. Rachel was happy to have someone to cook and clean for her, and selling the homestead had provided the family with some much-needed money.

To graduate from her program at Johns Hopkins, Rachel had to complete a research project. It was difficult to select a topic, but she finally decided to study catfish. Her focus would be on the temporary kidney that forms while the catfish embryo is developing. The research did not go well at first, and Rachel began to get frustrated. In a letter to Dorothy Thompson, she wrote, "I have made so many false starts along lines which yield no results, but that, I am learning, is the fate of most people."

During her years at Johns Hopkins, Rachel stayed in touch with her friends Mary Frye and Mary Scott Skinker by writing letters. At that time, long-distance telephone calls were expensive, and there was no such thing as e-mail. Writing letters was the best way for Rachel to keep in touch with her friends. Rachel wrote long, meaningful letters to her friends and acquaintances throughout her life. Fortunately, many of these letters have been preserved, and they give us a true glimpse into the mind of a great woman.

Returning to Writing

In 1932, Rachel finished her research project and graduated from Johns Hopkins with a master's degree in marine zoology. After spending that summer at Woods Hole, Rachel returned to Maryland and enrolled in a doctoral program at Johns Hopkins.

Rachel had hoped to finish the doctoral program quickly, but her father died unexpectedly in 1935. As a result, Rachel had to leave school and find full-time work. She had to support her sister, who had become very ill, her mother, and her two nieces—Marjorie and Virginia.

At first, Rachel had a hard time finding a job. Then she remembered Elmer Higgins—a man she had met at Woods Hole. Mary Scott Skinker had set up their first meeting in 1929. Higgins was now head of the Division of Scientific Inquiry at the Bureau of Fisheries in Washington, D.C. At their first meeting, Higgins had discouraged Rachel from pursuing a career in science. At their second meeting in 1935, however, he saw things differently.

Higgins was in charge of a project that involved the writing of fifty-two scripts for a radio series on marine life, which was to be called *Romance under the Waters*. He had asked several people to help him with the project but had been dissatisfied with their work. The scriptwriter he hired didn't understand science. The biologists wrote copy that was too technical. He needed writing that would be interesting to the average person but also scientifically accurate.

When Higgins hired Rachel, he said, "I've never seen a written word of yours, but I'm going to take a sporting chance." Rachel turned out to be the answer to Higgins's prayers—and, in a way, Higgins was an answer to Rachel's prayers too.

Years later, Rachel told an interviewer that her part-time job as a radio-script writer, which paid only $19.25 a week, had marked a turning point in her life. Since her early college days, Rachel had believed that she needed to choose between a career as a writer and a career as a scientist. "I thought I had to be one or the other," she later said. "It never occurred to me—or apparently to anyone else—that I could combine the two careers." After Higgins hired her, "It dawned on me that by becoming a biologist, I had given myself something to write about."

At the typewriter. Rachel's love of the natural world gave her much to write about.

UNDER THE SEA-WIND

Rachel hoped that once she proved herself as a writer to Higgins, he might help her find a permanent position. To prepare for that possibility, Mary Scott Skinker encouraged Rachel to take the civil service exam—a test that every full-time government employee must pass. Rachel received a high score on the test. When a position for a junior marine biologist opened up, Rachel got the job.

Rachel had indeed proven herself to Higgins. Her writing impressed him, and when the radio series ended, he asked her to adapt the scripts to create a series of government brochures on sea creatures. The brochures were going to be published together as a booklet, and Higgins requested that Rachel write a general introduction.

Rachel spent many hours on the introduction—she wanted to get it just right. When Higgins read the essay, which Rachel called "Worlds of Water," he was astounded. He gently told her that, although it was not right for the government publication, it would be a good piece for a magazine to publish. He suggested that she submit it to a magazine—*The Atlantic Monthly*. Rachel was delighted by Higgins's reaction, but she didn't take his advice. She put "Worlds of Water" in a desk drawer and wrote another introduction for the government booklet.

While Rachel was writing the radio scripts, she had decided to recast some of the information into a series of articles that might be appropriate for a newspaper. The first feature she submitted to the *Baltimore Sun* caught the attention of the editor in charge of the paper's Sunday supplement. For the next few years, Rachel continued to contribute articles to the Sunday *Sun*.

Encouraged by this success, Rachel gave some more thought to her essay, "Worlds of Water." She took it home to work on at night. She still didn't think it was ready to be published. When her sister, Marian, died in 1937, Rachel realized that she would now have to support the family by herself. She needed to find a way to earn more money. She finally finished revising "Worlds of Water" and submitted it to *The Atlantic Monthly.* If the magazine accepted the article, she told herself, the payment would come in handy.

The editors at *Atlantic Monthly* were impressed with Rachel's poetic descriptions of tube worms, sea slugs, and other ocean creatures. They agreed to publish the article but changed the title to "Undersea." When Quincy Howe, an editor at Simon & Schuster publishing company, read Rachel's article in the magazine, he was impressed too. He asked Rachel to write a book about the oceans and marine life.

The Writing Process

Rachel was thrilled to have the chance to write a book. For the next few years, she worked at her government job during the day and wrote the manuscript for *Under the Sea-Wind* at night. She had little time to spend with friends or family. Although she loved writing, she began to realize that it required great dedication and sacrifice.

Writing was hard work for Rachel, and she often had no one to talk to about her struggles. The frustration, loneliness, and isolation she first experienced while writing *Under the Sea-Wind* never left her. Years later, while addressing members of the American Association of University Women, she said:

> *Writing is a lonely occupation at best. Of course there are stimulating and even happy associations with friends and colleagues, but during the actual work of creation the writer cuts himself off from all others and confronts his subject alone. He moves in to a realm where he has never gone before—perhaps where no one has ever been. It is a lonely place, and even a little frightening. . . . I believe only the person who knows and is not afraid of loneliness should aspire to be a writer.*

Although Rachel had no human companionship during her late-night writing sessions, her cat, Buzzie, was always nearby. According to Rachel, he "used to sleep on my writing table, on the litter of

Writer's companion. During many long hours of writing, Rachel was often kept company by her devoted cat.

notes and manuscript sheets. On two of these pages I had made sketches, first of his little head drooping with sleepiness, then of him after he had settled down comfortably for a nap."

Under the Sea-Wind was published in 1941. The book contained three sections, describing life at the shore, life in the open seas, and life at the bottom of the sea. Rachel wanted to make her nonfiction writing flow like a novel. To achieve this, she thought about the techniques used by writers she had admired as a child. Some of those authors had given human characteristics to the imaginary animal characters in their stories to make them more engaging. Rachel did not want to turn the ocean creatures she was writing about into fictional characters, but she did sometimes describe them as "fearful" or suggest that they understood the concept of time. She felt that this would help her readers relate to the animals and their experiences.

Rachel rewrote and rewrote until she got it right. She later said, "Writing is largely a matter of . . . hard work, of writing and rewriting endlessly until you are satisfied that you have said what you want to say. . . . For me, that usually means many, many revisions." Sometimes, she asked her mother to read sections of the manuscript aloud so she could hear how it flowed. Rachel was pleased with the manuscript when she finally turned it in to Quincy Howe. To thank her mother for her lifelong support and devotion, Rachel dedicated *Under the Sea-Wind* to her.

Throughout her life, Rachel always said that *Under the Sea-Wind* was her favorite book. Authors often pour their heart and soul into their first major work—and this was certainly true for Rachel. She agonized over every word and every phrase. The book clearly shows her love of the natural world and the joy she felt while exploring it.

Although Rachel was pleased with her book, she did not know how the world would react to it. The thirty-four year-old author was thrilled when a reviewer from the *New York Times* wrote that the book was "skillfully written to read like fiction, but in fact a scientifically accurate account of life in the ocean and along the ocean shore." Other reviewers praised Rachel's lyrical, poetic writing style.

Disappointments

Although the critics liked *Under the Sea-Wind,* the book did not sell well. Rachel was disappointed. She had hoped that her royalty payments, which are based on a book's sales, would provide extra income for several years. When fewer than 1,500 copies sold during the book's first year in print, Rachel wrote a friend, "If one is to live even in part by writing, he may as well look at the facts. Except for the rare miracles where a book becomes a 'best seller,' I am convinced that writing a book is a very poor gamble financially." For the next few years,

Rachel decided to focus her efforts on writing magazine articles.

One of the most important reasons for the poor sales of the book was an event that was completely out of her control. Just one month after *Under the Sea-Wind* was shipped to bookstores, the Japanese bombed Pearl Harbor, Hawaii, and the United States entered World War II. In the midst of war, the last thing people were interested in reading was a book about the sea.

The war had another important effect on Rachel. In 1940, the U.S. Bureau of Fisheries—where Rachel worked—merged with the Biological Survey to form a new agency called the Fish and Wildlife Service. The agency was not considered essential to the war effort, and in 1942, Rachel's office was relocated to Chicago, Illinois. Rachel and her mother did not want to leave their home in Silver Spring, Maryland—but they had no choice. If Rachel did not move, she would lose her job.

Rachel moved to Chicago, but a year later, she was transferred back to Washington, D.C. She and her mother then moved into a house in Takoma Park, Maryland.

BUILDING A CAREER

In 1944, an illustrator named Kay Howe began working at the Fish and Wildlife Service. A year later, Kay's longtime friend, Shirley Briggs, also joined the staff. Rachel, Kay, and Shirley became great friends. Rachel enjoyed bird-watching or hiking with them on weekends. The three women often met with other Fish and Wildlife staff members at dinner parties to discuss science, current events, and other topics of interest. According to Shirley Briggs, "Rachel appreciated so many kinds of people, and was always glad to meet new ones

At Cobb Island, Virginia. No matter what projects she was working on, Rachel always had time for hiking and birdwatching.

and enter into whatever conversation or merriment was going on at these affairs."

By the mid-1940s, Rachel had been given several job promotions and had taken on a variety of new responsibilities. Although she enjoyed editing field reports, preparing press releases, and writing technical bulletins, she sometimes became frustrated with the work. At times, she considered leaving the Fish and Wildlife Service to work somewhere else as a writer or editor. She sent letters of inquiry to *Reader's Digest*, the New York Zoological Society, and the Audubon Society—but she had no luck.

Conservation in Action

After her promotions, Rachel's title had become Assistant Editor for the Division of Information at the Fish and Wildlife Service. She decided that her department should publish a series of booklets about national wildlife refuges—the large areas of land that are set aside by the U.S. government to protect rare plants and animals. Rachel's goal was to introduce readers to the many creatures living in each refuge and describe the role that each one played in its habitat.

For the next few years, Rachel traveled to many of the national wildlife refuges. She wanted to talk to the scientists who worked there and see the wildlife firsthand. Kay or Shirley accompanied her on many of these trips. Among the places Rachel visited were the Chincoteague Wildlife Refuge in Virginia, Parker River Wildlife Refuge in Massachusetts, Mattamus-

Wading at Chincoteague Wildlife Refuge. Rachel's research often led to firsthand experiences with wildlife.

keet Wildlife Refuge in North Carolina, Red Rock Lakes Refuge and National Bison Range in Montana, and Bear River Migratory Bird Refuge in Utah.

Rachel's office eventually published a total of twelve booklets in a series titled Conservation in Action. She wrote four herself and edited the others. In the introduction to one of the booklets, she wrote:

Wild creatures, like men, must have a place to live. As civilization creates cities, builds highways, and drains marshes, it takes away, little by little, the land that is suitable for wildlife. And as their spaces for living dwindle, the wildlife populations themselves decline.

Louis Halle, a naturalist who had met Rachel while she was working on the series, described her as "quiet, diffident, neat, proper, and without any affectation. She had dignity; she was serious . . . her voice was ever soft, gentle, and low." Although Rachel's professional demeanor was usually reserved and serious, her friends insist that there was another side to Rachel Carson. They remember her as fun-loving and mischievous.

A Second Book

By 1947, Rachel was giving serious thought to writing a second book. During World War II, the government had learned a great deal about the sea floor and, by the late 1940s, scientists were developing ideas about how the oceans had formed and changed over time. Many of these studies came across Rachel's desk at work, and she was intrigued.

In her free time, she had begun reading about the natural history of the ocean.

Rachel wanted to write a biography of the ocean. She wanted her book to present an overview of everything that scientists knew about the sea. She would weave together the work of biologists, zoologists, and oceanographers and include some seafaring history, mythology, and folktales. Most important, she would write it in a way that would engage the average reader. The book would teach science in an interesting and exciting manner and give people a new understanding and appreciation of the ocean and its vast array of creatures.

Despite her enthusiasm for the project, Rachel also had some misgivings. She remembered the long, lonely hours she had spent writing *Under the Sea-Wind.* She remembered, too, the disappointment that she felt when the book did not sell. Rachel wished she had someone in her life who really understood her as a person and the struggles she went through as a writer.

Rachel hoped to find such a kindred spirit in Ada Govern, a fellow nature lover and author she had corresponded with while writing an article on bird banding in 1945. As she wrestled with the idea of writing another book, she wrote the following to Ada:

> . . . *if I could choose what seems to me to be the ideal existence, it would be to live just by writing. But I have done far too little to dare risk it. And all the while my job with the service grows and demands more of me, leaving less time that I could put on my own writing. And as my salary increases little by little, it becomes even more impossible to give it up! That's my problem right now, and not knowing what to do about it, I do nothing.*

Ada understood Rachel's situation and tried to encourage the younger writer. In the end, however, it was a conflict that Rachel had to work out for herself.

By 1948, Rachel's research had picked up momentum. She was fully committed to her new book. She spent her evenings and weekends leafing through old books and skimming scientific papers. Whenever she found something of interest, she made careful notes. Later, Rachel described her research process:

. . . the backbone of the work was just plain hard slogging—searching in the often dry and exceedingly technical papers of scientists for the kernels of fact to weld into my profile of the sea. I believe I consulted, at a minimum, somewhat more than a thousand separate printed sources. In addition to this, I corresponded with oceanographers all over the world and personally discussed the book with many specialists.

During 1948 and 1949, Rachel spent many hours gathering information for her book, which she started to call *Return to the Sea*. Her research for the book had really begun years earlier, however—perhaps as early as 1929 when she spent her first summer in Woods Hole, Massachusetts. While working on the book, she told a friend, "I have been collecting material for this ocean book all my life. My mind has stored up everything I have ever learned about it as well as my own thoughts, impressions, and emotions."

Rachel decided that she would do everything in her power to make sure this second book sold better than her first. She knew that bad timing was one of the causes of the bad sales, but she also felt that the publisher should have done a better job promoting the book. She wanted to find a publishing company that would put a lot of energy into selling *Return to the Sea*. She also wanted to find a literary agent to help her with the business aspects of the publishing world.

She interviewed many agents and chose an energetic, savvy businesswoman named Marie Rodell. Marie handled Rachel's business affairs well and also became an important supporter and a loyal friend. Rachel was still searching for someone who could understand her as a person and as a writer, and Marie was able to fill this role too. After a month of working together, Rachel told Marie, "It is already proving to be a great comfort to have you."

When Rachel had created a detailed outline for the book and written a sample chapter, Marie started to search for the right publisher. In June 1949, Rachel signed a contract with Oxford University Press for the publication of *Return to the Sea*. The manuscript had to be finished by March 1950.

On the dock at Woods Hole. Rachel sometimes wrote and took notes while she spent time outdoors.

THE SEA AROUND US

As it was with *Under the Sea-Wind,* the writing process for the new book was slow and often frustrating. Rachel was a perfectionist. She kept writing and rewriting until she was completely satisfied with every sentence, every phrase, every word. Because Marie understood how much time and energy would be required to complete the book, she suggested that Rachel apply for a Eugene F. Saxton Memorial Fellowship. The fellowship would provide Rachel with money so that she could take time off from her job at the Fish and Wildlife Service.

In her application for the fellowship, Rachel described her new book as "an imaginative searching out of what is humanly interesting and significant in the life history of the earth's oceans; and the answering of questions thus raised in the light of the best available scientific knowledge." The scope and organization of the work was already beginning to solidify in Rachel's mind.

Final Touches

Rachel felt that to write a truly compelling book, she would need to experience, firsthand, the world below the ocean's surface. She wanted to go diving. Rachel and her friend Shirley headed for Florida.

Although the weather was bad on the day scheduled for the dive, Rachel knew she would probably not have another chance. She decided to take a quick undersea adventure to view the sea's rich array of fish, seaweed, and coral. She later described her experience: "I learned what the surface of the water looks like underneath and how exquisitely delicate and varied are the colors displayed by the animals of the reef, and I got the feeling of the misty green vistas of a strange, nonhuman world."

A few weeks later, Rachel headed to Woods Hole

for another ocean adventure. She and Marie spent ten days aboard the *Albatross III,* a fishing trawler that had been converted into a research vessel. Rachel wanted to learn more about deep-sea fish and the shape of the ocean floor. At first, the crew of fifty men was unhappy to have the two women on the boat, but Rachel and Marie ignored the noise of the nets' being released at night and endured the crew's teasing, so the men eventually accepted them.

Soon after she returned to Maryland, Rachel learned that she had been awarded a Saxton Fellowship. She took a few months off from her government job, but she continued to work as hard as ever. She was worried about meeting her March deadline. In February, it was clear that the book would not be finished in time.

Luckily, Marie was able to convince Oxford University Press to extend Rachel's deadline. The extra time eased some of Rachel's tension, and she began to approach the book with renewed enthusiasm. She got another boost when Marie told her that three prominent magazines—*The New Yorker, Science Digest,* and *The Yale Review*—were interested in publishing portions of the new book before it was printed.

By now, Rachel had returned to her job at the Fish

and Wildlife Service, but her work on the book progressed steadily through the spring and early summer. She finally finished the manuscript in late June 1950. She and her editor, Philip Vaudrin, then agreed that the book would be called *The Sea Around Us*.

A Third Book

After delivering her manuscript, Rachel took a well-deserved vacation with her niece Marjorie and her friend Shirley and then turned her attention back to her government job. Marie, however, was hard at work negotiating with the magazines that wanted to publish sections of *The Sea Around Us*. She was also discussing a new book project with Paul Brooks, an editor at Houghton Mifflin Publishing Company.

Houghton Mifflin was interested in a field guide to the animals that live along the coastal beaches of the United States. Rachel had discussed a similar concept with naturalist Edwin Way Teale a few years earlier and was very interested in pursuing the project.

During a weeklong trip to the North Carolina seashore in October, Rachel thought a great deal about the new book. She also thought about her lifelong fascination with the relationships among living things. She wanted to make sure that the seashore guide included these ideas and observations.

The Sea Around Us was not even printed yet, but Rachel was already thinking about a new book. That's how she was. Studying the natural world and writing about it was not just something she did to make money. She loved her work, and it gave her great joy.

To research *The Sea Around Us,* Rachel spent many hours reading in the library. Her next book allowed her to spend much more time outdoors. During the next few years, she would do research for her next book by walking along beaches and exploring tide pools up and down the Atlantic Coast.

Overcoming Obstacles

Rachel decided to apply for a Guggenheim Fellowship to support herself while she worked on the seashore guide. She felt that another leave of absence from her full-time job would make her writing proceed more quickly. As the responsibilities of her government position continued to expand, she found it increasingly difficult to focus on outside projects.

In 1949, Rachel had received another promotion.

She was made the editor in chief of all the U.S. Fish and Wildlife Service publications. As editor, she worked with authors to plan and write manuscripts and then edited and prepared the manuscripts for the printer. She also managed a staff of six in what she described as "the work of a small publishing company."

Rachel was very good at her job and widely admired by her coworkers. According to Bob Hines, an illustrator who worked closely with Rachel for

Always working. In addition to her own writing, Rachel served as editor of the U.S. Fish and Wildlife Service publications.

many years, "She knew how to get things done the quickest, simplest . . . [most] direct way. She had the sweetest, quietest 'no' any of us had ever heard. She had standards, high ones."

Working at such a demanding job during the day, writing at night, and helping her mother raise her nieces was taking its toll on Rachel, however. In the mid-1940s, Rachel began to suffer from appendicitis, shingles (a viral disease of the nerves), and a variety of other health conditions. In 1946, doctors had detected a lump in one of her breasts and removed it. Although it was not cancerous, it was a warning sign.

In 1950, doctors found a second lump in Rachel's breast. Once again, the tumor was removed and found to be benign. The doctors assured Rachel that no additional treatment was necessary. Meanwhile, Rachel's mother, who was in her early eighties, was also facing some medical problems, including surgery. Adding to Rachel's stress was her growing concern that the Korean War might affect the sales of *The Sea Around Us* in the same way World War II had affected the sales of *Under the Sea-Wind.*

In March 1951, however, Rachel finally received some good news. She learned that she would receive a Guggenheim Fellowship, which meant that she could take a full year off her job and focus all her energy on her next book.

Praise and Success

When *The Sea Around Us* was finally released in July 1951, Rachel waited breathlessly to see how the world would receive it. Within a few days, reviewers were gushing over the book. A reviewer from the *New York Times* said, "Once or twice in a generation does the world get a physical scientist with literary genius. Miss Carson has written a classic in *The Sea Around Us.*" Another critic praised her for "removing the mystery of the sea . . . while leaving the poetry." *The Sea Around Us* gave people a glimpse into the natural history and current state of the ocean. It described the creatures that inhabit the ocean and provided a thorough background of how the ocean had evolved over time. Although much of the information is now outdated, when the book was published, it included new information and ideas that captivated readers.

The book raced up the *New York Times* best-seller list. It was on the list for eighty-six weeks, holding the number-one position for thirty-two of them. The book was translated into thirty-two foreign languages and sold all over the world. A film-production company even bought the movie rights to *The Sea Around Us* and made an award-winning documentary based on Rachel's book.

Rachel could not believe her good fortune. Suddenly, people all over the world knew her name. Reporters wanted to interview her, colleges and universities wanted to give her honorary degrees, organizations all over the United States offered her speaking engagements. *The Sea Around Us* won numerous awards, but the crowning glory came in January 1952 when Rachel was awarded the National Book Award. That April, she also received the Burroughs Medal for excellence in nature writing.

In her acceptance speech for the National Book Award, Rachel referred to a comment made by one of her reviewers. "If there is poetry in my book about the sea," she said, "it is not because I put it in there but because no one could write truthfully about the sea and leave out the poetry."

At home in Maine. Rachel and her mother spent many summers along the Maine coast.

THE EDGE OF THE SEA

Rachel's yearlong leave of absence from the Fish and Wildlife Service began in June 1951. Not wanting to waste any time, she immediately headed for Woods Hole and spent several weeks there. The library at the Marine Biological Laboratory had all the resources she needed to do some thorough background research. Then, in the late summer, Rachel and her mother took a working vacation to Boothsbay, Maine. Maria and Rachel had first journeyed to Maine in 1946 and had returned every summer since. Both women loved the raw beauty of the Maine coast.

During their month-long stay, Marie Rodell and Bob Hines, an illustrator whose talent Rachel respected and whose companionship she adored, visited the Carsons. The two often spent entire days searching for and collecting the tide-pool creatures that Rachel wanted Bob to draw for her new book.

The manuscript was due in March 1953. Rachel planned to do library research in Maryland through the winter of early 1952 and then spend time on the road through September 1952. She wanted to visit Myrtle Beach in South Carolina, the Florida Keys, Woods Hole, and end the trip in Boothsbay. Bob and Rachel coordinated their schedules so that he could spend a few days at each site, giving him an opportunity to sketch the creatures she was studying.

Unfortunately, Rachel's plan got off to a bad start. Because of the overwhelming success of *The Sea Around Us,* she was constantly receiving phone calls from reporters who wanted to interview her. She was also buried in fan mail and requests for speaking engagements. In February 1952, she complained about these distractions in a letter to friend and naturalist Edwin Way Teale: "The longer *The Sea Around Us* stays at the top of the list, the greater, it seems, become the pressures of correspondence,

Knee-deep in research. Bob Hines joined Rachel in collecting the tide-pool animals he was to illustrate.

telephone calls, and interruptions of all sorts. Even just the labor of saying 'No' in a way that doesn't make people mad takes a good deal of nervous energy—and one cannot say no to everything."

Some of the publicity she received focused on her personality rather than her writing. Some reviewers expressed surprise that a woman had written *The Sea Around Us.* Others felt that only a burly, unattractive woman could be as knowledgeable as the book's author clearly was. The comments bothered Rachel, but she tried not to take them too seriously. As always, she remained a professional.

In Search of Structure

Her growing popularity was not the only reason that Rachel's work was progressing more slowly than she had expected. By the spring of 1952, she was struggling with how to organize the seashore guide.

Her first outline was organized in the same way as most field guides with the creatures themselves as the focus of the book. Rachel worried, however, that this structure would not achieve her goal—to emphasize the interrelationships among plants and animals in sea communities. She thought that perhaps there was a way to rework the book so that the habitats—not the creatures—were the main focus. She wasn't sure how to accomplish this, but hoped it would eventually become clear in her mind and proceeded with her travel plans.

Each day, Rachel awoke early to explore the coastal tide pools. Snails and starfish, crabs and barnacles, sea urchins and seaweed intrigued her. When she spotted an interesting creature, she gently scooped it up, placed it in a bucket of seawater, and examined it closely through a hand lens. Sometimes she also observed it under a stereomicroscope (a microscope with a lens for each eye). She made careful notes of what she saw, and then she always

Walking along the shore. Marjorie, Rachel's niece, often joined her aunt as she watched coastline creatures.

returned the creature to the exact spot where she had found it.

Rachel also explored tide pools at night, with the assistance of a flashlight, and on overcast days, decked out in rain gear. Sometimes she waded for hours in the icy tide pools near Ocean Point, Maine. She would get so absorbed in her work that she didn't even notice the cold. On at least one occasion,

The Edge of the Sea **69**

her body went numb, and Bob Hines had to pull her out of the water and wrap her in blankets.

Rachel's leave of absence from the Fish and Wildlife Service was scheduled to end in the middle of her six-month journey along the Atlantic Coast. For the first time in her life, however, Rachel was not worried about having a full-time job. The royalty payments from *The Sea Around Us* were larger than Rachel had expected. *Under the Sea-Wind* had been re-released in April, and its sales were also strong. The success of these two titles made Rachel financially independent. She knew that if she invested her money wisely and spent it carefully, she could devote the rest of her life to writing.

In June 1952, Rachel resigned from her government position. She also returned a portion of her Guggenheim Fellowship. Her money problems were now a thing of the past.

In the fall, Rachel purchased land in West Southport, Maine, and built a small cottage where she and her mother could spend their summers. In many ways, Rachel's life had never been better. Although she should have been happy, she spent her days and nights worrying. She was still struggling with the structure of the seashore guide. She finally admitted to her agent, Marie, that she would not be able to finish the book by the March deadline.

Marie got an extension from the publisher, but Rachel was still unhappy. She tried to enjoy a trip to Florida in December, but all she could think about was the book. Finally, in June 1953, Rachel had an idea. For the third time, she completely restructured the book. The book would emphasize ecosystems rather than individual creatures. She would present the three basic types of shorelines—rocky beaches, sandy beaches, and coral reefs—and the community of living things found in each.

A New Friend

Rachel finally had a plan, but she was still many months away from completing her manuscript. She was depressed and needed encouragement. Although Marie had helped while Rachel was writing *The Sea Around Us,* the book's success had somewhat changed the women's relationship. Once again, Rachel was yearning for someone who understood her as a person and as a writer.

In the summer of 1953, Rachel and her mother moved into their Maine cottage. Soon after, they were visited by their neighbors, Dorothy and Stan

Freeman. Rachel and Dorothy quickly became friends.

Dorothy and Stan lived in West Bridgewater, Massachusetts, but they spent their summers in Maine. Rachel and Dorothy discovered that they shared a passion for nature, especially the ocean. Rachel could also freely discuss the challenges of her writing and her fears about her mother's declining health. Rachel also enjoyed Stan's companionship. She began using his photographs of ocean creatures in her lectures and speeches. As time passed, Rachel began to think of Dorothy and Stan as members of her family.

Rachel spent the summer exploring the tide pools around Sheepscot Bay, answering fan mail, and visiting with friends and family. She also happily spent time with her niece Marjorie and Marjorie's year-and-a-half-old son, Roger. In the fall, she was ready to get back to Maryland to work on the seashore guide.

During the fall and winter months, Dorothy and Rachel wrote long letters to each other. As Rachel battled with her manuscript, Dorothy's letters came as a welcome distraction. In one letter, Rachel told Dorothy, "The lovely companionship of your letters

Special friendship. Dorothy Freeman and her husband provided advice and companionship to Rachel for many years.

has become a necessity to me . . . you are helping me more than you can imagine."

As time passed and their friendship grew, Rachel came to depend more and more on Dorothy's sound advice and comforting nature. She wrote:

> *I don't suppose anyone really knows how a creative writer works (he or she least of all, perhaps!) or what sort of nourishment his spirit must have. All I am certain of is this: that it is quite necessary for me to know that there is someone who is deeply devoted to me as a person, and who also has the capacity and the depth of understanding to share, vicariously, the sometimes crushing burden of creative effort, recognizing the heartache, the great weariness of mind and body, the occasional black despair it may involve—someone who cherishes me and what I am trying to create as well.*

Rachel and Dorothy remained close for the rest of their lives.

"She's Done It Again"

Rachel finished her book in March 1955. Paul Brooks, her editor at Houghton Mifflin, was pleased—and relieved—to finally receive the manuscript. He had been waiting patiently for two years. As soon as he read the first draft, he knew the book had been worth the wait. He said, "I am convinced that it contains some of the best writing that you have ever done and that there are passages here superior to anything in *The Sea Around Us*."

In one section of the book, she beautifully describes the forces responsible for changes in water level along the shore:

For no two successive days is the shoreline precisely the same. Not only do the tides advance and retreat in their eternal rhythms, but the level of the sea itself is never at rest. It rises or falls as the glaciers melt or grow, as the floor of the deep ocean basins shifts under its increasing load of sediments, or as the earth's crust along the continental margins warps up or down in strain and tension. Today a little more land may belong to the sea, tomorrow a little less. Always the edge of the sea remains an elusive and indefinable boundary.

Rachel was thrilled with Paul's reaction to her manuscript. As with her two previous books, she had been nervous about how this book would be received. Together, the author and editor decided to call this book *The Edge of the Sea*. Rachel had lovingly dedicated the book to Dorothy and Stan Freeman, "who have gone down with me into the low-tide world and have felt its beauty and its mystery."

Others were impressed too. The editors of *Reader's Digest* wanted to publish a condensed version of the entire book. Magazine editor William Shawn wanted to publish a portion of *The Edge of the Sea* in *The New Yorker*. According to Marie Rodell, when Shawn called to work out the financial arrangements, his first words were, "She's done it again."

Despite editorial praise, Rachel still worried about how the critics and the public would respond. Would *The Edge of the Sea* live up to their expectations?

Rachel need not have worried. Soon after the book hit the bookstores, reviewers were as impressed as Paul Brooks and William Shawn had been. A review in *The New York Times* echoed William Shawn's words exactly: ". . . the main news is that she has done it again." *The Edge of the Sea* rocketed up the best-seller list and stayed there for twenty-three weeks.

NEW DIRECTIONS 7

Rachel had planned to take time off from writing after she finished *The Edge of the Sea,* but by the end of 1955, she was already beginning to consider several new projects. She had many offers, including a book on evolution and an anthology (collection) of stories, essays, and poems about the sea. Both projects seemed like something Rachel would enjoy, but the first project she wanted to work on was an article for *Woman's Home Companion.*

The editors of the magazine wanted a piece that would teach children how to

Honor and fame. Rachel received a number of honorary degrees throughout her career.

observe and appreciate the natural world. The project gave Rachel an opportunity to include stories about the adventures that she and her now four-year-old grandnephew, Roger, had shared while he was visiting her in Maine.

The article, titled "Help Your Child Wonder," was published in July 1956. Rachel told her readers: "A child's world is fresh and new and beautiful, full of wonder and excitement. It is our misfortune that for most of us that clear-eyed vision, that true instinct for what is beautiful and awe-inspiring, is dimmed and even lost before we reach adulthood."

When Dorothy read the piece, she wrote to Rachel saying, ". . . the public is going to find a new you—the one I've known from the start, the you of the starry eyes, the elfin you, the whimsical, fanciful you who appealed so much to me."

As always, Rachel was grateful for the praise the article received, but didn't let it interfere with her work. She was already thinking about her next project. While delivering a speech to the American Association of University Women, she told her audience: "No writer can stand still. He continues to create or he perishes. Each task completed carries its own obligation to go on to something new. I am always more interested in what I am about to do than in what I have already done."

The Lost Woods

Rachel was now spending a lot of time caring for her mother, who was suffering from arthritis, and her niece Marjorie, whose diabetes was worsening. To escape from her nursing duties, she spent as much time as she could exploring the nearby woods with Dorothy.

Rachel and Dorothy began to call the area the "Lost Woods." Both were enchanted by the exquisite beauty and the diversity of living creatures they found there. They felt that this magical place should be preserved forever. Eventually, Rachel decided to do whatever was necessary to make sure the land was preserved as a wildlife sanctuary. She could not afford to buy the land herself, so she considered founding an organization that could use donations from members to purchase the plot.

Rachel's commitment to saving the Lost Woods had completely revived her spirit. Suddenly, her life seemed to have a purpose. Throughout the fall, she dreamed about schemes for saving the Lost Woods. By December, after several promising new offers came her way—including a children's version of *The Sea Around Us*—she began to fantasize about earning enough money to buy the Maine plot herself.

Full of enthusiasm, she wrote to Curtis Bok, a Pennsylvanian judge who had sent Rachel fan mail about a year earlier. After Rachel had learned that Curtis's father had created two wildlife sanctuaries in Florida, the two continued to correspond. She was now anxious to let Curtis know about her own efforts to save Lost Woods, which she described as "a cathedral of stillness and peace. . . . a treasure of a place to which I have lost my heart completely."

Curtis recommended that before Rachel devote any more time and energy to the project, she contact the landowner to find out whether he had any interest in selling the land. Rachel followed Curtis's advice, but by the time she received the owner's disappointing reply several months later, Rachel's life had changed completely.

Life's Demands

In January 1957, her niece Marjorie died of pneumonia and complications resulting from diabetes. There was no one else to care for Roger, Marjorie's five-year-old son, so Rachel—then forty-nine years old—agreed to become Roger's adoptive mother. Rachel had a full-time housekeeper, but caring for her young grandnephew and her eighty-eight-year-old mother took a lot of time and energy. In addition, Rachel was also constructing a new house in Silver Spring and building an addition on her cottage in Maine. With the demands of these responsibilities, Rachel found little time to write. She decided to put the sea anthology on hold and focus on short-term projects.

By the fall, Rachel was settled into her new home and Roger had started school. She agreed to write an article on America's seashores for *Holiday* magazine. Although Rachel wanted to write an article that made people understand how few pristine beaches were left, the magazine was more interested in a descriptive piece that drew on material she had covered in *The Edge of the Sea*. Rachel told the editors: "I cannot write about the shores I love without pointing out their peril. . . . For it is only as people are informed of dangers that threaten such priceless regions that they can be saved." As a compromise, Rachel wrote an article that described many of her favorite beaches, but included a final section that discussed the need to protect and preserve coastal areas.

As time passed, Roger became more and more needy. He wanted to be with Rachel constantly, which made it difficult for her to find time to write the article. Even though "Our Ever-Changing Shore" was due in January 1958, she did not complete it until mid-February. Months earlier, she had spoken to Paul Brooks about writing a full-length book on a similar topic, but now she saw how difficult it would be to write another book. Once again, she decided to stick with magazine work.

Speaking Out

About this time, Rachel received a letter from Olga Owens Huckins. The two women had been corresponding since 1951 when Rachel wrote to thank Olga, who was then the literary editor of the *Boston Post,* for her excellent review of *The Sea Around Us.* Olga lived on a bird sanctuary in Duxbury, Massachusetts, and was deeply committed to protecting wildlife and their habitats.

Olga's letter contained a clipping from the *Boston Herald.* A naturalist and organic gardener named Beatrice Trum Hunter had written a letter to the newspaper's editor. She was enraged by the spraying of pesticides near her home in Hillsboro, New Hampshire. In her letter, she described the extensive damage that the pesticide dichloro-diphenyl-trichloro-ethane (DDT) had done near her home. By writing the letter, Beatrice hoped to show her support for a group of Long Islanders who were trying to put an end to spraying in their own area. The group had taken their case to court. They wanted all spraying to stop until the long-term effects of DDT were discovered.

Olga had also written a letter to the *Boston Herald.* She told readers that the spraying had killed a number of birds on her sanctuary. "All of these birds died horribly," she explained. "Their bills were gaping open, and their splayed claws were drawn up to their breasts in agony." Then she continued, "Air spraying where it is not needed or wanted is inhuman, undemocratic, and probably unconstitutional. For those of us who stand helplessly on the tortured earth, it is intolerable."

This was not the first time Rachel had heard about the harmful affects of DDT. In 1939, a Swiss chemist named Paul Muller discovered that the chemical compound has potent insect-killing properties. After conducting a series of experiments, he declared that DDT was harmless to humans and other mammals. During World War II, DDT was used to dust soldiers for lice and to combat mosquitoes that spread malaria and typhoid. Soon, DDT was pronounced the "savior of mankind," and Paul Muller was awarded a Nobel Prize.

By 1945, however, some government studies were beginning to suggest that DDT might not be as harmless as Paul Muller believed. At that time, Rachel was working at the Fish and Wildlife Service, so she saw these early studies and read them with interest. She tried to convince several magazine edi-

Dangerous pesticide. DDT was sprayed on crops for many years before its safety was called into question.

tors to publish an article on the topic, but they were not interested. They were afraid that chemical manufacturers would no longer pay to advertise in their magazines if they published such an article.

Olga Huckins's letter now reawakened Rachel's interest in DDT. Once again, Rachel tried to find a magazine that would publish an article about DDT, but editors were still scared. Although Rachel had promised herself that she would not take on a new book project, she felt a strong need to educate the American public about the dangers of DDT and other chemical insecticides. Remembering those early months of 1958, Rachel recalled, "The more I learned about the use of pesticides, the more appalled I became. I realized that here was the material for a book. What I discovered was that everything which meant most to me as a naturalist was being threatened, and that nothing I could do would be more important."

Paul Brooks, Rachel's editor at Houghton Mifflin, showed great interest in the project—a book that Rachel was then calling *Man Against the Earth*. Although she dreaded the months of hard work ahead of her, Rachel felt she had no choice. When she told Dorothy about her new book, she said, "Knowing what I do, there would be no future peace for me if I kept silent."

SILENT SPRING 8

Rachel asked Edwin Diamond, an editor for *Newsweek* magazine, to work with her on the new book. She thought that having a coauthor might relieve some of the burden. Soon, it became clear that the partnership wasn't going to work out, however, so she decided to hire a research assistant and write the book herself.

Rachel signed a contract with Houghton Mifflin in May 1958, and the manuscript was due in January 1959. Like her two previous books, parts of this new work would also appear in *The New Yorker* magazine. Rachel spent the next few months hunting for scientific articles and corresponding with dozens of scientists who studied pesticides.

In November, Maria Carson had a stroke, and one month later she died of pneumonia. Rachel was devastated. Except for the years that Rachel had spent in college and graduate school, mother and daughter had lived together for Rachel's entire life. Rachel had a great deal of trouble concentrating on her work, and she knew that she would not meet her January deadline. She eventually realized, however, that finishing *Man Against the Earth* was the best way for her to honor her mother's memory. She told a friend, "while gentle and compassionate, [Mamma] could fight fiercely against anything she believed wrong, as in our present Crusade! Knowing how she felt about that will help me return to it soon, and to carry it through to completion."

Moving Forward

By February 1959, Rachel had returned to her piles of research and correspondence. With the help of her assistant, Bette Haney, Rachel's research was going fairly well. At first, Rachel and Bette were easily able to request the information they wanted from government offices and libraries. When officials found out what Rachel was writing about, however, they became less cooperative, and many tried to block her requests. Because Rachel had worked for the government for so long, she was often able to find other ways to get the materials she needed. Many other government scientists wanted the truth to be told too.

Rachel wrote identical letters to Paul Brooks and William Shawn, assuring the editors that she was on the right track. "It is now possible to build up, step by step, a really damning case against the use of these chemicals as they are now inflicted upon us." Paul was glad to hear that Rachel was making progress, but he was nervous. *The Edge of the Sea* was delivered two years late, and he hoped that this book would not take her as long to complete.

For most of the summer, Rachel was distracted from her work on *Man Against the Earth.* Roger developed a respiratory infection and needed care. She also had to complete work on some other small projects that were long overdue. Troubling changes in her relationship with Dorothy Freeman also distracted Rachel. Dorothy was not as supportive of this new book as she had been of *The Edge of the Sea.* She was concerned about how Rachel's long hours of work and little sleep would affect her health.

Rachel soon found ways to get herself back on track. She turned to two new friends for the support she needed—budding authors Lois Crisler and Beverly Crisler. Her friendship with Marie Rodell also deepened. By fall, Rachel was overburdened with unanswered letters and again behind schedule on her book. She decided to hire Jeanne Davis as a secretary and research assistant. Rachel was very pleased with Jeanne's work. She told Paul Brooks, "If I had set out to make someone up I could hardly have done better! The problem of the moment seems to be to find some hormone that will split both Mrs. Davis and me into twins!"

Physical Challenges

By the end of the year, Rachel felt she might finish the book by summer. But, once again, she was delayed by circumstances that were out of her control. In January 1960, she developed a serious ulcer. Dorothy was not surprised when she heard about Rachel's ulcer. She blamed it on years of stress and anxiety. She told Rachel, "You, I think, are the type—the person who, on the surface, keeps calm, shows no

Sharing time with the birds. As she grew older, Rachel's health began to fail, but she always made the effort to be outdoors.

emotion, and goes along apparently unruffled with all the tensions bottled up inside. There have been times when, if I had been you, I would have screamed!"

As the ulcer was starting to heal, Rachel developed pneumonia and a sinus infection. In March, she had several new lumps in her breast removed. According to her doctors, one of the tumors was "suspicious," and she had surgery to remove the breast. After the operation, her doctor assured Rachel that radiation therapy was not necessary. She did her best to continue working during her long, painful recovery.

By late spring, she had finished the first drafts of most chapters and sent them to experts for their review. In a letter to Paul Brooks she said, "You are the most patient of editors, and often I am aware that I must try even your patience sometimes. I guess all that sustains me is a serene inner conviction that when at last the book is done, it is going to be built on an unshakable foundation."

During the summer, Rachel spent time revising *The Sea Around Us* for a new edition. She also wrote an article about the sea for *Johns Hopkins Magazine*. In the fall, she revised the *Man Against the Earth* manuscript, incorporating the comments the experts had made.

In November, Rachel discovered a strange lump between her ribs. After an examination and a series of tests, Rachel's doctor recommended that she immediately begin radiation therapy. Rachel had cancer, and it was spreading. Although the treatments made her very sick, she continued to work. Throughout 1961, a variety of radiation-related ailments slowed her progress. Finally in January 1962, she sent the manuscript to her editors.

Brave, New Ideas

Rachel's manuscript contained a series of essays that clearly explained how DDT and other pesticides

A man dressed as Death. Rachel's warnings about DDT led to many public protests about the pesticide.

affect the natural world. She showed that human efforts to destroy the pests responsible for Dutch elm disease also killed robins and warblers. She explained that spraying programs designed to kill mosquitoes and gypsy moths harmed bald eagles, and that the controls for Japanese beetles killed rabbits, muskrats, and squirrels. Rachel also pointed out

Silent Spring

that, often, some insects develop a resistance to the chemicals being used to destroy them—so, over time, the spraying does more harm and less good.

She wrote that pesticides "have the power to kill every insect, the 'good' and the 'bad,' to still the song of birds and the leaping of fish in the streams, to coat the leaves with a deadly film, and to linger on in soil—all this though the intended target may be only a few weeds or insects."

Rachel agreed that pesticides can help farmers produce more and better crops, but she explained that they can also harm a variety of other animals—including humans. Rachel argued that the potent chemicals should be used more carefully and sparingly. She wanted people to know that, although it was once considered the "savior of man," DDT and other pesticides could in fact be the "killer of man."

Residues of these chemicals linger in soil to which they may have been applied a dozen years before. They have entered and lodged in the bodies of fish, birds, reptiles, and domestic and wild animals so universally that scientists carrying on animal experiments find it almost impossible to locate subjects free from such contamination.

They have been found in fish in remote mountain lakes, in earthworms burrowing in soil, in the eggs of birds—and in man himself. For these chemicals are now stored in the bodies of the vast majority of human beings, regardless of age. They occur in the mother's milk, and probably in the tissues of the unborn child.

The World Reacts

William Shawn called Marie Rodell as soon as he finished reading Rachel's book. He was very pleased with it and planned to publish parts in *The New Yorker* that June. Rachel was relieved by Shawn's response. As always, she needed to know that her editors were pleased with her work. Paul Brooks was also satisfied. He suggested that the new book be called *Silent Spring*.

Rachel and Paul were both worried about how chemical manufacturers would react to *Silent Spring*. Rachel had not originally intended to criticize a billion-dollar industry, but the evidence against them—and many government agencies—was staggering. She and Paul thought that the companies might try to take legal action, but the solid list of sources that she included at the back of the book provided facts to support every word she had written. In fact, before the book came out, one company threatened to sue both Rachel and Houghton Mifflin. But the author and publisher would not be stopped.

When *Silent Spring* was released in September 1962, some reviewers praised it as a "godsend," others claimed that it contained "downright errors" and "scary generalizations." Even though the chemical industry and some scientists criticized Rachel, the public took her seriously. People bought the book—and read it. Within two weeks of publication, *Silent Spring* was number one on the *New York Times* bestseller list. The book was later translated into many languages and sold throughout the world.

In April 1963, the TV news show *CBS Reports* broadcast a report on the controversial book. The host, Jay Mullen, had spent months doing research and interviewing many people. During his program, the scientists who represented the chemical industry came across as angry and defensive. Rachel seemed relaxed and composed. In the show's closing statement, Rachel told viewers, "We still talk in terms of conquest. We still haven't become mature enough to think of ourselves as only a very tiny part of a vast and incredible universe. Now I truly believe that we in this generation must come to terms with nature, and I think we're challenged, as mankind has never been challenged before, to prove our maturity and our mastery, not of nature but of ourselves."

Many Americans took her advice to heart. People began to form organizations to question government policies regarding the environment. President John F. Kennedy was so influenced by Rachel's book that he created a special panel of the Science Advisory Committee to investigate pesticides. Eventually, the panel's findings supported Rachel's claims. Rachel Carson died of breast cancer on April 14, 1964—but her legacy lives on. As one newspaper editor said, "A few thousand words from her, and the world took a new direction."

A Far-Reaching Legacy

For most Americans, *Silent Spring* was a startling wake-up call. People were shocked to learn that the spraying of pesticides—a practice endorsed by their own government—could be slowly killing them.

The publication of *Silent Spring* started a worldwide discussion about how humans should take care of nature. Could scientists develop ways of controlling pests without harming other living things? Peo-

Remembering Rachel Carson. In 1970, the Rachel Carson National Wildlife Refuge was named to honor her.

ple wanted them to try. Before the book was published in 1962, any product could be sold to the public until, and unless, government scientists proved that it was dangerous. In 1964, new legislation was passed that made manufacturers more responsible for the safety of their products. According to this new law, they had to actually prove the product was safe before it could be made available to the public.

In 1970, the U.S. government created the Environmental Protection Agency (EPA), and in 1972, the EPA banned the use of DDT in the United States. More recently, Congress passed the Clean Air Act to protect the air we breathe, and the Clean Water Act to protect the water we drink. These changes might have been greatly delayed—or perhaps never have happened at all—if Rachel Carson had not written *Silent Spring*.

Despite all the efforts that the United States has made in passing laws to protect the environment, new threats arise all the time. Although DDT was banned many years ago, it was quickly replaced by new types of pesticides—some that are even more poisonous. Scientists at the Smithsonian Institution's Migratory Bird Center estimate that 67 million birds still die every year from exposure to pesticides on American farms. Clearly, we need to find solutions to the problems created by the pesticides and other toxins that endanger us and our environment.

As a child, Rachel watched the growth of industry pollute the Allegheny Valley and destroy her rural home and her parents' financial prospects. As an adult, she saw firsthand the dangers facing our nation's wildlife refuges. She also witnessed the destruction of many of America's pristine beaches. Perhaps better than anyone else in her generation,

Earth Day in Central Park. Because of Rachel Carson's work, more people are now better educated about preserving the natural world.

Rachel understood the hidden costs of technology and progress. Because of her work as a respected author and scientist, people throughout the world—then and today—have heard her message and taken action.

TIMELINE

1907	Rachel Carson born on May 27 in Springdale, Pennsylvania
1918	Publishes four stories in *St. Nicholas Magazine*
1929	Graduates from Pennsylvania College for Women; visits the Marine Biological Laboratory in Woods Hole, Massachusetts, for the first time
1932	Receives master's degree in marine zoology from Johns Hopkins University
1935	Writes series of radio scripts for the U.S. Bureau of Fisheries
1937	"Undersea" published in *The Atlantic Monthly*
1941	Publishes *Under the Sea-Wind*
1949	Becomes editor in chief of all U.S. Fish and Wildlife Service publications
1951	Publishes *The Sea Around Us;* wins the National Book Award and Burroughs Medal for excellence in nature writing
1955	Publishes *The Edge of the Sea*

1956	Publishes "Help Your Child Wonder" in *Woman's Home Companion*
1957	Adopts Roger, her niece Marjorie's son, after Marjorie dies
1962	Publishes *Silent Spring*
1964	Dies of breast cancer on April 14

HOW TO BECOME A BIOLOGIST

The Job

Biology can be divided into many specialties. The biologist, who studies a wide variety of living organisms, has interests that differ from those of the chemist, physicist, and geologist, who are concerned with nonliving matter. Biologists, or *life scientists*, may be identified by their specialties. Following is a breakdown of the some of the kinds of biologists and their specific fields of study.

Aquatic biologists study animals and plants that live in water and how they are affected by their environmental conditions, such as the salt, acid, and oxygen content of the water and temperature, light, and other factors.

Biochemists study the chemical composition of living organisms. They attempt to understand the complex reactions involved in reproduction, growth, metabolism, and heredity.

Botanists study plant life. Some specialize in plant biochemistry, the structure and function of plant parts, and identification and classification, among other topics.

Ecologists examine such factors as pollutants, rainfall, altitude, temperature, and population size in order to study the distribution and abundance of organisms and their relation to their environment.

Entomologists study insects and their relationship to other life forms.

Geneticists study heredity in various forms of life. They are concerned with how biological traits such as color, size, and resistance to disease originate and are transmitted from one generation to another. They also try to develop ways to alter or produce new traits, using chemicals, heat, light, or other means.

Marine biologists specialize in the study of marine species and their environment. They gather specimens at different times, taking into account tidal cycles, seasons, and exposure to atmospheric elements, in order to answer questions concerning the overall health of sea organisms and their environment.

Microbiologists study bacteria, viruses, molds, algae, yeasts, and other organisms of microscopic or submicroscopic size. Some microorganisms are useful to humans; they are studied and used in the production of food, such as cheese, bread, and tofu. Other microorganisms have been used to preserve food and tenderize meat. Some microbiologists work with microorganisms that cause disease. They work to diagnose, treat, and prevent disease. Microbiologists have helped prevent typhoid fever, influenza, measles, polio, whooping cough, and smallpox.

Today, they work on cures for AIDS, cancer, cystic fibrosis, and Alzheimer's disease, among others.

Wildlife biologists study the habitats and the conditions necessary for the survival of birds and other wildlife. Their goal is to find ways to ensure the continuation of healthy wildlife populations, while lessening the impact and growth of civilization around them.

Requirements

High School   High school students interested in a career in biology should take English, biology, physics, chemistry, Latin, geometry, and algebra.

Postsecondary Training   Prospective biologists should also obtain a broad undergraduate college training. In addition to courses in all phases of biology, useful related courses include organic and inorganic chemistry, physics, and mathematics. Modern languages, English, biometrics (the use of mathematics in biological measurements), and statistics are also useful. Courses in computers will be extremely beneficial. Students should take advantage of courses that require laboratory, field, or collecting work.

Nearly all institutions offer undergraduate training in one or more of the biological sciences. These vary from liberal arts schools that offer basic majors in botany and zoology to large universities that permit specialization in areas such as entomology, bacteriology, and physiology at the undergraduate level.

The best way to become a biologist is to earn a bachelor's degree in biology or one of its specialized fields, such as anatomy, bacteriology, botany, ecology, or microbiology. For the highest professional status, a doctorate is required. This is particularly true of top research positions and most higher-level college teaching openings. Many colleges and universities offer courses leading to a master's degree and a doctorate.

Certification or Licensing A state license may be required for biologists who are employed as technicians in general service health organizations, such as hospitals or clinics. To qualify for this license, proof of suitable educational background is necessary.

Other Requirements
Biologists must be systematic in their approach to solving the problems that they face. They should have probing, inquisitive minds and an aptitude for biology, chemistry, and mathematics. Patience and imagination are also required since they may spend much time in observation and analysis. Biologists must also have good communication skills in order to effectively gather and exchange data and solve problems that arise in their work.

Exploring
Students can determine their interest in the work of the biologist by taking courses in the field. Laboratory assignments, for example, provide information on techniques used by the working biologist. Many schools hire students as laboratory assistants to work directly with a teacher.

Part-time and summer positions in biology or related areas are particularly helpful. Beginning college and advanced high school students may find employment as laboratory aides or hospital orderlies or attendants. Despite the menial nature of these positions, they afford a useful insight into careers in biology. Student science training programs (SSTPs) allow qualified high school students to spend a summer doing research under the supervision of a scientist.

Employers

Marine biologists might find employment with the U.S. Department of Interior, the U.S. Fish and Wildlife Service, and the National Oceanic and Atmospheric Administration. They may also find employment in nongovernmental agencies, such as the Scripps Institution of Oceanography in California and the Marine Biological Laboratory in Massachusetts. Microbiologists can find employment with the U.S. Department of Health and Human Services, the Environmental Protection Agency, and the Department of Agriculture, among others. They may also work for pharmaceutical, food, agricultural, geological, environmental, and pollution control companies.

Starting Out

Biologists who are interested in becoming teachers should consult their college placement offices. Public and private high schools and an increasing number of colleges hire teachers through the colleges at which they studied. Private employment agencies also place a significant number of teachers. Some teaching positions are filled through direct application.

Biologists interested in private industry and nonprofit organizations may also apply directly for employment. Major organizations that employ biologists often interview college seniors on campus. Private and public employment offices frequently have listings from these employers.

Special application procedures are required for positions with government agencies. Civil service applications for federal, state, and municipal positions may be obtained by writing to the agency involved and from high school and college guidance and placement bureaus, public employment agencies, and post offices.

Advancement

In a field as broad as biology, numerous opportunities for advancement exist. To a great extent, however, advancement depends on the individual's level of education. A doctorate is generally required for college teaching, independent research, and top-level administrative and management jobs. A master's degree is sufficient for some jobs in applied research, and a bachelor's degree may qualify for some entry-level jobs.

With the right qualifications, the biologist may advance to the position of project chief and direct a team of other biologists. Many use their knowledge and experience as background for administrative and management positions. Often, as they develop professional expertise, biologists move from strictly technical assignments into positions in which they interpret biological knowledge.

The usual path of advancement in biology, as in other sciences, comes from specialization and the development of the status of an expert in a given field. Biologists may work with professionals in other major fields to explore problems that require an interdisciplinary approach.

Work Environment
The biologist's work environment varies greatly depending upon the position and type of employer. One biologist may work outdoors or travel much of the time. Another wears a white smock and spends years working in a laboratory. Some work with toxic substances and disease cultures—strict safety measures are observed.

Earnings
Salaries for all biological scientists range from $27,930 to over $86,020, with a median salary of $46,140, as reported by the U.S. Department of Labor. In 1999, biologists with bachelor's degrees who worked for the federal government earned average salaries of $56,000 a year; ecologists averaged $57,100; microbiologists averaged $62,600; and geneticists, $68,200.

Outlook
The U.S. Department of Labor predicts a faster-than-average increase in employment of biologists through 2008, although competition will be stiff for high-paying jobs, and government jobs will be less plentiful.

TO LEARN MORE ABOUT BIOLOGISTS

Books
Camenson, Blythe, and Stephen E. Lambert, et al. *Great Jobs for Biology Majors*. Lincolnwood, Ill.: VGM Career Horizons, 1999.

Collard, Sneed B. *A Whale Biologist at Work*. Danbury, Conn.: Franklin Watts, 2000.

Wendt, Jennifer. *Marine Biologist*. Mankato, Minn.: Capstone Press, 2000.

Winter, Charles A., and Kathleen Belikoff. *Opportunities in Biological Science Careers*. Lincolnwood, Ill.: VGM Career Horizons, 1998.

Websites
American Institute of Biological Sciences
http://www.aibs.org
The home page for the AIBS

American Society for Microbiology
http://www.asmusa.org
The home page for the American Society for Microbiology

Where to Write
American Physiological Society
Education Office
9650 Rockville Pike
Bethesda, MD 20814-3991
For a career brochure, career-related articles, and a list of institutions that award academic degrees with a major in physiology

National Institutes of Health
National Center for Research Resources
Building 12A, Room 4003
Bethesda, MD 20892
For information on specific careers in biology

National Aquarium in Baltimore
Department of Education and Interpretation, Pier 3
501 East Pratt Street
Baltimore, MD 21202-3194
For information on careers in the marine sciences

HOW TO BECOME A WRITER

The Job

Writers are involved with the expression, editing, promoting, and interpreting of ideas and facts. Their work appears in books, magazines, trade journals, newspapers, technical studies and reports, company newsletters, radio and television broadcasts, and even advertisements.

Writers develop ideas for plays, novels, poems, and other related works. They report, analyze, and interpret facts, events, and personalities. They also review art, music, drama, and other artistic presentations. Some writers persuade the general public to choose certain goods, services, and personalities.

Writers work in the field of communications. Specifically, they deal with the written word for the printed page, broadcast, computer screen, or live theater. Their work is as varied as the materials they produce: books, magazines, trade journals, newspapers, technical reports, company newsletters and other publications, advertisements, speeches, scripts for motion-picture and stage productions, and for radio and television broadcasts.

Prose writers for newspapers, magazines, and books do many similar tasks. Sometimes they come up with their own idea for an article or book and sometimes they are assigned a topic by an editor. Then they gather as much information as possible about the subject through library research, interviews, the Internet, observation, and other methods. They make notes from which they gather material for their project. Once the material has been organized, they prepare a written outline. The process of developing a piece of writing involves detailed and solitary work, but it is exciting.

When they are working on an assignment, writers submit their outlines to an editor or other company representative for approval. Then they write a first draft of the manuscript, trying to put the material into words that will have the desired effect on their readers. They often rewrite or polish sections of the material, always searching for just the right way of getting the information across or expressing an idea or opinion. A manuscript may be reviewed, corrected, and revised numerous times before a final copy is submitted.

Writers for newspapers, magazines, or books often specialize in a specific subject. Some writers might have an educational background that allows them to give a critical interpretation or analysis. For example, *a health* or *science writer* typically has a degree in biology and can interpret new ideas in the field for the average reader.

Screenwriters prepare scripts for motion pictures or television. They select—or are assigned—a subject, conduct research, write and submit a plot outline or story, and discuss possible revisions with the producer and/or director. Screenwriters may adapt books or plays for film and television. They often collaborate with other screenwriters and may specialize in a particular type of script.

Playwrights write for the stage. They create dialogue and describe action for comedies and dramas. Themes are sometimes adapted from fictional, historical, or narrative sources. Playwrights combine action, conflict, purpose, and resolution to tell stories of real or imaginary life. They often make revisions even while the play is in rehearsal.

Continuity writers prepare material for radio and television announcers to introduce or connect various parts of their programs.

Novelists and *short-story writers* create stories for books, magazines, or literary journals. They use incidents from their own lives, from news events, or from their imagination to create characters, settings, and actions. *Poets* create narrative, dramatic, or lyric poetry for books, magazines, or other publications, as well as for special events such as commemorations.

Requirements

High School   High-school courses that are helpful for a writer include English, literature, foreign languages, general science, social studies, computer science, and typing. The ability to type and familiarity with computers are almost requisites for positions in communications.

Postsecondary   Competition for work as a writer almost always demands the background of a college education.

Many employers prefer people who have a broad liberal arts background or a major in English, literature, history, philosophy, or one of the social sciences. Some employers prefer communications or journalism training in college. Occasionally a master's degree in a specialized writing field may be required. A number of colleges and schools offer courses in journalism, and some of them offer courses in book publishing, publication management, and newspaper and magazine writing.

In addition to formal education, most employers look for practical writing experience. If you have worked on high-school or college newspapers, yearbooks, or literary magazines, you will make a better candidate. Work for small community newspapers or radio stations, even in an unpaid position, is also an advantage. Many book publishers, magazines, newspapers, and radio and television stations have summer internship programs. These provide valuable training if you want to learn about the publishing and broadcasting businesses. Interns do many simple tasks, such as running errands and answering phones, but some may be asked to perform research, conduct interviews, or even write some minor pieces.

Writers who specialize in technical fields may need degrees, concentrated course work, or experience in their subject areas. This usually applies to engineering, business, and the sciences. Also, a degree in technical communications is now offered at many colleges.

If you want a position with the federal government, you will be required to take a civil service examination and meet specific requirements, according to the type and level of the position.

Other Requirements Writers should be creative and able to express ideas clearly, have broad general knowledge, be skilled in research techniques, and be computer-literate. Other assets include curiosity, persistence, initiative, resourcefulness, and an accurate memory. For some jobs—on a newspaper, for example, where the activity is hectic and the deadlines are short—the ability to concentrate and produce under pressure is essential.

Exploring

As a high-school or college student, you can test your interest and aptitude in the field by working as a reporter or writer on school newspapers, yearbooks, and literary magazines. Various writing courses, workshops, and books help you to sharpen your writing skills.

Small community newspapers and local radio stations often welcome contributions from outside sources, although they may not have the resources to pay for them. Jobs in bookstores, magazine shops, and even newsstands can help you become familiar with the various publications.

Information on writing as a career may also be obtained by visiting local newspapers, publishers, or radio and television stations. You may interview some of the writers who work there. Career conferences and other guidance programs often have speakers on the field of communications from local or national organizations.

Employers

Nearly one-third of salaried writers and editors work for newspapers, magazines, and book publishers, according to the *Occupational Outlook Handbook*. Many writers work for advertising agencies, in radio and television broadcasting, or in public relations firms. Others work on journals and newsletters published by business and non-profit organizations. Other employers include government agencies and film-production companies.

Starting Out

Experience is required to gain a high-level position in this field. Most writers start out in entry-level jobs. These jobs may be listed with college placement offices, or you may apply directly to publishers or broadcasting companies. Graduates who have previously served internships with these companies often know someone who can give them a personal recommendation.

Employers in the communications field are usually interested in samples of your published writing. These may be assembled in an organized portfolio or scrapbook. Bylined or signed articles are more helpful than those whose source is not identified.

A beginning position as a junior writer usually involves library research, preparation of rough drafts for a report, cataloging, and other related writing tasks. These are generally carried on under the supervision of a senior writer.

Advancement

Most writers start out as editorial or production assistants. Advancement is often more rapid in small companies, where beginners learn by doing a little of everything and may be given writing tasks immediately. In large firms, however, duties are usually more compartmentalized. Assistants in entry-level positions do research, fact-checking, and copyrighting, but it generally takes much longer to advance to writing tasks.

Promotion into a more responsible position may come with the assignment of more important articles and stories, or it may be the result of moving to another company. Employees in this field often move around. An assistant in one publishing house may switch to an executive position in another. Or a writer may advance by switching to a related field: for example, from publishing to teaching, public relations, advertising, radio, or television.

Freelance or self-employed writers may advance by earning larger fees as they widen their experience and establish their reputation.

Work Environment

Working conditions vary for writers. Although the workweek usually runs thirty-five to forty hours, many writers work overtime. A publication that is issued frequently has more deadlines closer together, which creates greater pressures. The work is especially hectic on newspapers and at broadcasting companies, which operate seven days a week. Writers often work nights and weekends to meet deadlines or to cover a late-developing story.

Most writers work independently, but often they must cooperate with artists, photographers, rewriters, and advertising people. These people may have widely differing ideas of how the materials should be prepared and presented.

The work is sometimes difficult, but writers are seldom bored. Each day brings new and interesting problems. The jobs occasionally require travel. The most difficult aspect is the pressure of deadlines. People who are the most content as writers enjoy and work well under deadline pressure.

Earnings

In 1998, median annual earning for writers were $36,480 a year, according to the *Occupational Outlook Handbook*. Salaries range from $20,920 to $76,660.

In addition to their salaries, many writers earn some income from freelance work. Part-time freelancers may earn from $5,000 to $15,000 a year. Freelance earnings vary widely. Full-time established freelance writers may earn up to $75,000 a year.

Outlook

Employment in this field is expected to increase faster than the average rate of all occupations through 2008. The demand for writers by newspapers, periodicals, book publishers, and nonprofit organizations is expected to increase.

The major book and magazine publishers, broadcasting companies, advertising agencies, public relations firms, and the federal government account for the large number of writers in cities such as New York, Chicago, Los Angeles, Boston, Philadelphia, San Francisco, and Washington, D.C. Opportunities in small newspapers, corporations, and professional, religious, business, technical, and trade publications can be found throughout the United States.

TO LEARN MORE ABOUT WRITERS

Books

Fletcher, Ralph B. *A Writer's Notebook: Unlocking the Writer within You.* New York: Camelot, 1996.

Janeczko, Paul B. *How to Write Poetry.* New York: Scholastic, 1999.

Krull, Kathleen. *Lives of the Writers: Tragedies, Comedies.* Austin: Raintree/Steck-Vaughn, 1998.

New Moon Books Girls Editorial Board. *Writing: How to Express Yourself with Passion and Practice.* New York: Crown, 2000.

Reeves, Diane Lindsey. *Career Ideas for Kids Who Like Writing.* New York: Facts On File, 1998.

Stevens, Carla. *A Book of Your Own: Keeping a Diary or Journal.* New York: Clarion, 1993.

Websites
Creative Writing for Teens
http://teenwriting.about.com
Tips, news, activities, a chat room, and a selection of young authors' works

4Writers
http://www.4writers.com
Support for professional and aspiring writers, plus information about conferences, artists' colonies, and the top creative writing programs

Writer's Digest
http://www.writersdigest.com
Features daily writing and publishing updates, plus information about the best places to get published

Where to Write
National Association of Science Writers
P.O. Box 294
Greenlawn, NY 11740
516/757-5664
For information on writing and editing careers in the field of communications

National Conference of Editorial Writers
6223 Executive Boulevard
Rockville, MD 20852
301/984-3015
For information about student memberships available to those interested in opinion writing

PEN American Center
568 Broadway
New York, NY 10012-3225
Helps foster writers of literary works and provides awards, grants, and support

Tallwood House
MSN 1E3
George Mason University
Fairfax, VA 22030
Provides support for writers and a directory of writing programs

Writers Guild of America
7000 West Third Street
Los Angeles, CA 90048
For information about this organization that represents writers of all kinds

TO LEARN MORE ABOUT RACHEL CARSON

Books

Brooks, Paul. *Rachel Carson: The Writer at Work*. San Francisco: Sierra Club Books, 1998.

Carson, Rachel. *Always, Rachel: The Letters of Rachel Carson and Dorothy Freeman, 1952–1964. The Story of a Remarkable Friendship*. New York: Beacon Press, 1996.

Carson, Rachel. *The Edge of the Sea*. Boston: Houghton Mifflin, 1955.

Carson, Rachel. *The Sea Around Us*. New York: Oxford University Press, 1951.

Carson, Rachel. *Silent Spring*. Boston: Houghton Mifflin, 1962.

Carson, Rachel. *Under the Sea-Wind*. New York: Oxford University Press, 1952.

Finch, Robert and John Elder (ed.) *The Norton Book of Nature Writing*. New York: W. W. Norton, 1990.

Lear, Linda. *Witness for Nature.* New York: Henry Holt, 1997.

Wadsworth, Ginger. *Rachel Carson: Voice for the Earth.* Minneapolis: Lerner, 1992.

Website
Rachel Carson
www.rachelcarson.org
This site features biographical information about Rachel Carson as well as links to a variety of other sites.

Interesting Places to Visit
Rachel Carson Homestead
Springdale, Pennsylvania
724/274-5459

INDEX

Page numbers in *italics* indicate illustrations.

Albatross III (research vessel), 57
Allegheny River, 14–15, 22, 99
The Atlantic Monthly magazine, 38–39

Baltimore, Maryland, 30
"Battle in the Clouds" (short story), 19–21
Biological Survey, 44
biologists
  career advancement, 108–109
  career exploration, 106–107
  educational requirements, 105–106
  employers of, 107
  employment outlook, 109
  job description, 103–105
  salaries, 109
  work environment, 109
Boston Herald newspaper, 83

Boston Post newspaper, 83
Briggs, Shirley, 45, 56, 58
Brooks, Paul, 58, 74, 76, 82, 86, 89–90, 92

Carson, Maria (mother), 13, 16–17, *18*, 65, 88
Carson, Marian (sister), *12*, 13, 18, 31–32, 39
Carson, Rachel, *8*, *12*, *18*, *20*, *24*, *26*, *31*, *36*, *46*, *48*, *54*, *60*, *64*, *67*, *69*, *78*, *91*
  birth of, 13
  childhood of, *12*, 14, 17, *18*, 19–20, *20*, 22
  death of, 97
  education of, 22, 25–34
  health of, 61, 90–92
Carson, Robert, Jr. (brother), *12*, 13, 18
Carson, Robert, Sr. (father), 13–14, 17, 34
Chatham College. *See* Pennsylvania College for Women (PCW).

125

chemical manufacturers, 11, 85, 95
coastal tide pools, 68
Conservation in Action booklet series, 48–49

Davis, Jeanne, 90
Diamond, Edwin, 87
dichloro-diphenyltrichloro-ethane (DDT), 83–85, *85*, 92–94, *93*, 99

ecologists, 11, 104
The Edge of the Sea (book), 11, 75–77, 82, 89
Environmental Protection Agency (EPA), 98–99
Eugene F. Saxton Memorial Fellowship, 55, 57

Fish and Wildlife Service, 44–45, 47, 55, 57–58, 60, *60*, 65, 70, 84
Freeman, Dorothy, 71–73, *73*, 75–76, 79–80, 89
Freeman, Stan, 71–72, 75–76

Govern, Ada, 50–51
Guggenheim Fellowship, 59, 62, 70

Halle, Louis, 49
Haney, Bette, 88
"Help Your Child Wonder" (magazine article), 78–79
Hines, Bob, 60, 66, *67*, 70

Houghton Mifflin Publishing Company, 58, 74, 86–87, 96
Huckins, Olga Owens, 83, 85

Johns Hopkins Magazine, 92
Johns Hopkins University, 30–31, 33–34

literary reviews, 43, 62, 76, 83
"Lost Woods" (forest), 80

Man Against the Earth (Rachel Carson), 86, 88–89, 92
Marine Biological Laboratory, 30, 65
"The Master of the Ship's Light" (short story), 25–26
"A Message from the Front" (short story), 21
Migratory Bird Center, 99
Monongahela River, 14–15
National Book Award, 63

New York Times newspaper, 43, 96
The New Yorker magazine, 57, 76, 87, 95

oceans, 27, 31, 49–50, 52, 56–57, 72. *See also* seashore.
"Our Ever-Changing Shore," 82

Pennsylvania College for Women (PCW), 22–23, 25, *26*, 29
pesticides, 9, 85–86, *85*, 92–94, 97, 99
pollution, 10, 15–16, 99

Rachel Carson National Wildlife Refuge, *98*
Return to the Sea (Rachel Carson), 52–53
Rodell, Marie, 53, 66, 71, 76, 90, 95
Roger (grandnephew), 78, 81, 89
Romance Under the Waters (radio series), 34–35

Science Digest magazine, 57
The Sea Around Us (book), 11, 58, 61–63, 67, 70–71, 80, 83, 92
The Sea Around Us (documentary), 63
seashore, 59, *67*, 68, *69*, 82. *See also* oceans.
Shawn, William, 76, 89, 95
Silent Spring (book), 9–10, 95–97, 99
Skinker, Mary Scott, 28–29, 33–34, 37
St. Nicholas Magazine, 19, 21, 25

Teale, Edwin Way, 58, 66
Tennyson, Alfred Lloyd, 30

U.S. Bureau of Fisheries, 44
U.S. Fish and Wildlife Service. *See* Fish and Wildlife Service.
Under the Sea-Wind (book), 11, 39–42, 50, 70
"Undersea" (essay), 39

Vaudrin, Philip, 58
Virginia (niece), 34

Woman's Home Companion magazine, 77
Woods Hole, Massachusetts, 30, *31*, 34, *54*, 56–57
"Worlds of Water" (essay), 38–39
writers
  career advancement, 117–118
  career exploration, 116
  educational requirements, 114–116
  employers of, 116–117
  employment outlook, 119
  job description, 112–114
  salaries of, 119
  work environment, 118

The Yale Review magazine, 57

ABOUT THE AUTHOR

Melissa Stewart earned a bachelor's degree in biology from Union College and a master's degree in science and environmental journalism from New York University. She has been writing about science and nature for almost a decade.

Like Rachel Carson, Melissa spent many hours of her youth exploring the woods around her parents' home. As a native New Englander, she made her first trip to Cape Cod before she could walk and has many fond memories of West Dennis Beach. Because Melissa shares Rachel Carson's two major interests—a love of nature and a desire to write about it—she greatly enjoyed researching and writing this book.